Million Dollar Turtles

Wayne Rollins and Gary Bentley

TEKTON PUBLISHING

ISBN: 978-0-89098-751-3

©2015 by Tekton Publishing

P.O. Box 40526

Nashville, TN 37204

Distributed by 21st Century Christian

2809 12th Ave. South

Nashville, TN 37204

Cover design by Jonathan Edelhuber

Printed in the United States of America

Table of Contents

Dedication

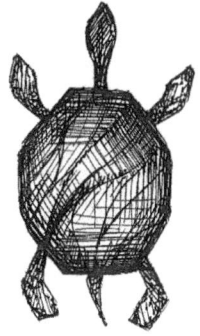

To our families and especially Thomas Rollins, Wayne's father, who is a true example of what this book is about. Thomas is deeply dedicated to this country, his family, and God. He is an excellent example of the kind of person who built this great nation. Thomas spent his life making life better for the country and for those around him. If not for the example he set, we simply could not have written this book.

Thomas Rollins

Acknowledgments

Million Dollar Turtles is a book reflecting common sense through our own real-life stories. We acknowledge everyone who has worked with us along our paths and all the people mentioned in this book.

Stacey Owens, our editor, converted our thoughts and words into a meaningful manuscript. She demonstrated patience and kindness throughout numerous revisions and rewrites. We appreciate both her technical skill and her insight with suggestions on content to delete as well as content to amplify or clarify.

We also owe a great debt to Matthew McInteer and Mark McInteer, our publishers. They guided us in the presentation of the chapters, supplied an abundance of publication options, and provided legal counsel.

Ms. Hannah Glass provided sketches throughout the book. We have a difficult time drawing straight lines with a ruler! Hannah, who attends church where Wayne is a member, is an aspiring Illustrator, and we are honored to provide her a platform in which to enter the profession.

Finally, we could have done none of this without the support of our families. During the time we devoted to this book, our families tolerated preoccupied and part-time husbands and fathers. We especially thank our wives for putting up with us through the years as we struggled to become successful in our respective professions.

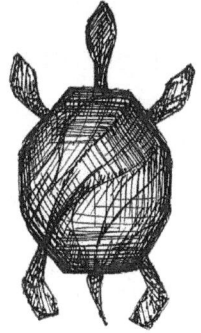

Foreword

I t all started on a trip to a professional conference in October 2011 where a colleague and I were scheduled to present a paper. Although this professional colleague was my boss, he was also a peer with whom I had traveled numerous times. We knew each other's travel habits; specifically, he likes an aisle seat while I prefer a window seat when flying. That meant a seat would be between us . . . filled or vacant.

Do you believe in divine providence? On this particular day, a traffic accident had occurred on I-65 south of Nashville, Tennessee. The accident caused a detour, which almost caused the Turtleman and his family to miss their flight. Well, I believe in God, and I believe the detour caused Gary, the Turtleman, to sit between my colleague and me. The flight was full, and Gary had little seat choice since he and family were the last ones to board. His family sat together but were short one seat. Upon reflection, the seat between my colleague and me was the only seat left on the flight.

Regardless, Gary and I were seated together preparing for a three-hour flight. Gary was cordial but quite reserved. He probably thought I was too inquisitive since I began asking about what he did, where he lived, and making other social chitchat. When I inquired about what he did for a living, he seemed to enjoy seeing me struggle to guess what he "grew" on his farm.

Thus was the beginning of a conversation that intrigued me for three hours. Wanting others to be just as intrigued, I invited Gary to speak to two of my classes at Middle Tennessee State University the following fall semester. When I introduced him, I reflected on asking him so many questions. The more I found out about Gary's turtle farm, the more questions popped into my mind. When Gary went to the podium, he told the classes that our initial meeting had been more like an interrogation.

I was attracted to Gary's story for many reasons, which I've detailed in this book. The main attraction, however, was the parallel between Gary and my father, Thomas Rollins. As Gary shared his turtle story with me (through much prodding and prying on my part), I felt like I was in a parallel dimension. Daddy had experienced so many things Gary had encountered and would continue to encounter.

Entrepreneurs go through so many obstacles and barriers. Gary sensed that my admiration and respect for Daddy were also extended to him as he shared those obstacles with me. By the end of the flight, Gary had provided me his contact information, and I'd tentatively scheduled a trip to his turtle farm.

On July 3, 2012, I was honored to take my wife and my parents to Killen, Alabama, to visit Gary and his turtle farm. Gary is a natural teacher, so the speaking engagement to visit my classes was solidified. Gary wanted to co-author this book, which is another indicator he is a teacher as well as an entrepreneur. Both Gary and I get excited to tell stories, give illustrations, and share knowledge. Both of us like to be successful, and we deeply desire to help others become successful, too.

Together, we're an entrepreneur and an academic who have teamed up to help you along your journey to become more successful in the work world and in your life.

How would you like the recipe for success? Well, we would like to give it to you, but we can't. We can tell you what has worked for us, but that may not work for you. People have to develop their own special recipe, the recipe that works best for them. We hope to do three things in this book: give you some ingredients that you can use in your master recipe; share stories of things we've seen and insights we've learned along the way to encourage you to watch others, for good or poor examples, so that you can add more ingredients to your recipe as you travel through life; and to increase your vision of the big picture. Only you know where you want to go, so be the first one to get there.

_____

Gary Bentley

_____

Wayne Rollins

CHAPTER 1

It's the Small Things
(or Avoid the Cracks)

When you're a business owner, you wear many different hats. You're the chief cook and bottle washer — you do it all. You have a vision/dream, you have a plan, and you're willing to do the work. You must manage your time, finances, and all the business resources to accomplish your goals. You're responsible for everything. With such a wide span of responsibility, there's certainly the possibility that you'll forget a detail or two!

One year I was busy "growing" turtles. I had learned the incubation time for eggs, the temperature needed for proper incubation, how to harvest the eggs, where different turtle species lay eggs, the breeding period, the laying period, and many more facts one must know.

So much work had gone into getting the right ratio of males to females, creating the proper "nest" environment for the turtles, harvesting the eggs, etc. that I viewed buying a thermometer as one of the easier tasks I needed to perform.

I went to a reputable store and purchased a $2.00 thermometer so that I could regulate the temperature to properly heat the eggs during incubation. Caring for thousands of future turtles was an exciting and important job! I watched the temperature closely and made the proper adjustments in the heating equipment and eagerly awaited the birth of thousands of tiny turtles.

Strangely, the turtles began hatching earlier than I had learned they would during my studies. It was exciting seeing those shells crack!

Thousands of turtles making their way into the world is a sight to see, and I had played a small part in this creation. So much hard work had gone into harvesting the eggs. Now the birthing was in full swing!

Time passed and I began to notice only the cracks. The turtles weren't breaking through their shells. Why weren't they coming out of their shells? After some additional research, I learned that the symptom of eggs hatching too fast caused by too much heat is that the turtles are too weak to get out of the shell. How could I have given them too much heat? I had monitored the eggs closely and calibrated my heat with the thermometer. The thermometer! Could the problem really have been so simple?

I purchased another thermometer and placed it in the room only to learn that the $2.00 thermometer I had purchased was 10 degrees off. Though I thought I had been incubating them at a cozy 82 degrees, I had actually been baking them at 92 degrees. This small detail of purchasing a $2.00 thermometer (and not validating it) had cost me about $30,000! That was a big deal to me, because I needed the money to help grow the business. It was also a big psychological-let down. It was hard doing all that work to wind up with so little in return.

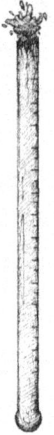

Looking back, that one little problem has saved me many headaches over the years and prevented lots of other mistakes. We must learn from the small problems to avoid being destroyed by larger ones. When we learn not to avoid problems but begin to welcome them as challenges that will strengthen us, we learn to check the details and eventually overcome detail challenges.

One thing you'll find on the turtle farm today is lots of thermometers — at least two in every room!

A good friend of mine who's a retired veterinarian told me a story about working with the chicken industry when chicken breasts and chicken strips became popular. Geneticists started breeding the chickens to have larger breasts so that they could cater to the market demands. They didn't realize they were breeding a five- to six-pound chicken with legs designed to support a three- to four-pound bird. It became an obvious problem when farmers started raising chickens with legs that couldn't support their weight.

With just a little thought, you can provide many examples of the importance of details. You can have the greatest automobile in the world with the biggest engine; however, if you neglect to change the oil, the engine will be ruined. Many forest fires have been started by a red ember that campers thought they had extinguished.

Vince Lombardi once said, "Practice does not make perfect. Only perfect practice makes perfect." I'm confident the coach was careful about details during practice. Learn the importance of details and conquer the small ones. You'll prevent future mistakes!

"It's the little details that are vital.
Little things make big things happen."
~ John Wooden

"Details create the big picture."
~ Sanford I. Weill

CHAPTER 2

Timing Makes a Difference
(or The Right Time to Stick Your Neck Out)

I had a friend in his upper 60s who wanted to build a cabin to rent for $500 a month. The initial construction cost was about $100,000. After doing some math, I figured it would take him 20 years to recover his initial investment; he would be 87 years old. Furthermore, the $100,000 cost didn't include upkeep, taxes, insurance, and other unforeseen costs, including lack of rent due to vacancy.

Often when someone asks me about a project like this, I ask whether it's something they want to do or if it's something in which they're interested to make money? If it's something you're doing for a hobby, then you should go for it. If it's something you're doing to make money, it isn't a good idea."

Age should be a critical factor when considering timing. Realistically, how long will it take to overcome start-up costs? The idea of the rental cabin for someone who is 27 is different from someone in their late 60s.

A lady recently asked me, "When do you know when to give up on a new business that is failing?" She and her husband had started a trucking business a year or two beforehand. She said they'd discussed what to do at certain points if the business was doing well, but they hadn't discussed what to do if the business was losing money. My advice has always been that if someone has an idea derived from passion, "Stay long enough to give it a chance, but not long enough to go bankrupt."

Their business is an example of detail (*see chapter 1*). They purchased an older truck, which likely doesn't get the same gas mileage as more recent models. Although the older model may have saved them some money up front, one has to consider that if a truck gets eight miles per gallon instead of 10, that's an extra 20 percent in fuel costs. A cost/benefit analysis should be made to determine how many miles it would take to offset the additional up-front cost of a truck with better mileage. How long to "stay the course" always involves timing.

Timing is also crucial with regard to your family status. Children demand much of our time and attention, and the ages of children are significant factors when building a business. If you're married, is your spouse involved in the business? Many people with great aspirations have been defeated because of timing, not because of their work ethic, idea, or business.

How important is time? Let me ask you another question. What if you knew someone who ran for political office 10 times and was defeated each time? Well, I must admit I would advise the individual to get out of politics! Thankfully, I was never asked since this individual lived in another era of U.S. history.

Unfortunately, this individual didn't just fail in his bids for office. Often considered lazy by some in his family, he failed in business before eventually finding political success. How could a person fail so many times while seeking election, fail in business, and fail to keep one of his jobs? Could timing really have so much influence?

Abraham Lincoln is considered by many people to be one of the best presidents in U.S. history. Accounting for only the failures listed above (he had several more), timing is the only logical explanation for his failures to supreme successes.

Abraham Lincoln failed in business and declared bankruptcy. Many people have failed in business and declared bankruptcy who had great ideas, great work ethics, and great businesses — only to have them at the wrong time.

None of us controls the economy; however, we can learn from its timing (cycles). Businesses have cycles which are predictable — to a degree. We can't predict exactly when things will happen; however, we can anticipate them. When interest rates are low, they will eventually rise. When the stock market declines, it will eventually rise. The converse, however, is also true. When prices, interest rates, stock market, and other factors are high, they will decline … eventually. Of course, the key is timing.

In the early 1990s when I was in the mussel shell business, the price of shells doubled and then tripled, which in turn, made the number of those who worked as mussel shell catchers jump from a few hundred to a few thousand. This price change had two effects: the market was suddenly flooded with shells, which caused the price to collapse, and the ones who stayed in the business after the price dropped had a difficult time making a living. Why? The mussel shell population had been depleted when the prices doubled and tripled.

My farming friends tell me examples that reflect the importance of timing. They say if corn prices are high in a given year, then the following year a large percentage of farmers plant corn and plant less soybean and cotton. Then, there is a large supply of corn, which may push the price down and a smaller supply of cotton and soybeans, which can raise the price of those commodities. This may be human nature, but it may not be the best business practice.

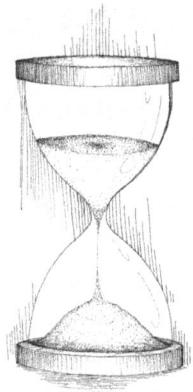

I'm familiar with the scrap metal industry since my dad and grandfather were scrap metal collectors, so I learned about this business from a young age. In the last decade, China and other countries have increased their demand for raw materials, which caused the price of scrap metals to increase three or four times. This price increase inflated the number of individuals who were collecting scrap metals to sell to scrap yards. Land owners who had scrap metal lying around for years suddenly decided to sell it or allow collectors to get it. The end results were the same: The number of people collecting skyrocketed and the available scrap metal was depleted. The supply was severely decreased, but the number of people trying to find it was higher. Now, the people collecting scrap metal are having a much harder time finding scrap metal because there is little left to be found.

Study your history, and learn to anticipate events. Timing makes a difference!

"I learned that we can do anything, but we can't do everything . . . at least not at the same time. So think of your priorities not in terms of what activities you do, but when you do them. Timing is everything."

~ Dan Millman

"The big picture doesn't just come from distance; it also comes from time."

~ Simon Sinek

CHAPTER 3

Tools Are Important
(or Use the Best Equipment)

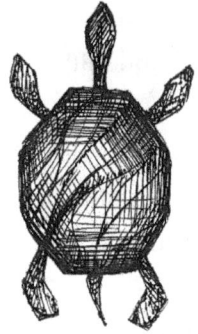

There are numerous advantages for a young boy who's raised in a small country town. I remember an event that happened more than 50 years ago like it happened last month. The memory is clear because I learned a valuable lesson at that event that ironically, I wasn't even seeking to learn.

In the small town where I was raised, the men folk gathered once during the late summer to cut the grass on a field in the middle of our community. All the children and teenagers genuinely appreciated this grass being cut since that's where we played baseball, softball, football, badminton, horseshoes, Frisbee, and was where we flew kites. Of course, the kite flying ended in March and virtually every other activity ended as the grass grew taller and taller. Having the grass cut meant that we could start the games again!

My daddy, who was in his 30s, had a slingblade like the other younger and middle-aged men. The younger men grouped together, so they got my attention. The tool they used was the new slingblade that one could swing in two directions. Everybody had this unique tool and seemed to be most proud to own the newest thing in grass cutting.

But away from that crowd was an older man named Charlie. Everyone knew Charlie. He always had a big "chaw" of tobacco in his jaw, and he always wore overalls. What grabbed my attention about Charlie was his sickle. That's right. Charlie didn't use a new slingblade, which made me feel sorry for him. My initial impression was that he was an old man with an old, outdated tool, so I pitied him.

As the work began, the younger group of men swung with such fervor — in two directions. Their swings were so rapid! Tall grass reeds with seeds bowing flew everywhere! Then there was poor Charlie with his old sickle; his pace was much slower, but I noticed it was quite consistent. I also noticed he had a pattern: He would cut a swath that consumed a complete half circle, take one step, and repeat the process. His cuttings weren't flying everywhere but fell gently to the ground.

My curious observation taught me a valuable lesson. A significant difference exists between activity and productivity. Those younger men were active, but Charlie was productive. The frantic pace of the younger men caused them to need to stop for rest several times, but Charlie never tired. And he was two to three times their age! As I recall, Charlie cut more grass than the five or six younger men combined; furthermore, his cuttings were much neater and flatter on the ground.

I walked away that day with a renewed appreciation for Charlie — and old proper tools. You must realize that this was a big lesson to me, especially since I'm severely mechanically challenged.

Tools are important and can drastically increase your productivity, but the lack of proper tools can dramatically decrease your productivity. Furthermore, how you use your tools and equipment can make all the difference in the world.

When I was in the mussel shell business and started diving, the other divers were using dive bags they bought from the dive shop. Those bags were designed with a rope for divers to hang around their necks, which would drag the bottom as divers basically crawled across the river bottom. Visibility was poor that deep in the river, and divers had

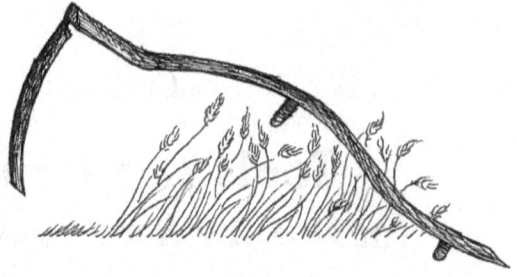

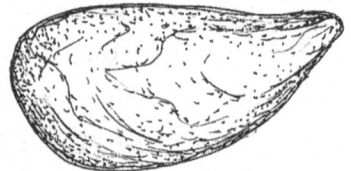

to crawl to be able to see or feel for the shells. Visibility was so bad at times some people who were claustrophobic couldn't dive.

The dive shop mussel bag had a plastic ring in its throat to hold the bag open so divers could put the shells in the opening. I quickly found multiple problems with this store-bought bag. As the bag filled up with mussel shells, it was hard to drag across the river bottom, which slowed me down. The bag would hang on rocks, sticks, and other debris, which took time to get free again. Because of the friction of dragging the bag on the river bottom debris, that bag would develop holes quickly. Consequently, all of that dragging tired me quickly.

So I designed my own bag. It had a stainless steel ring in the throat to hold the mouth open for putting shells in quickly. The ring was also designed to hook over the back of my weight belt, so the bag would rest on the back of my legs as I crawled across the river bottom.

By hanging the bag on my weight belt on the back of my legs, the bag didn't drag, which allowed me to move more quickly across the river bottom. Not dragging the bag across the bottom of the river bed prevented holes from being worn in the bag.

With the bag setting on the back of my legs as the shells filled the bag, all the weight would be on my legs rather than on my neck, so I wasn't slowed down. For precaution, I attached a small rope with a hook to the bag so I wouldn't lose it. I also had another small rope with a hook hanging from my boat into the water so I could fill a bag, climb my air hose to the surface, and hang the bag on the side of the boat. I could reach another self-designed bag and return to the river bottom quickly. This procedure and equipment gave me more work time on the bottom. Most divers only carried one bag. When they filled it, they had to surface, climb into their boat, take off their weight belt, stop the compressor, and go through their shells.

They wasted so much time in their boats! My system allowed me to make longer, multiple dives and have energy to work longer hours. Even after getting more shells and moving faster across the bottom, I could work longer than the other divers.

Those divers who worked around me always wondered how I retrieved more shells than they every day. They said, "You can see better, you don't smoke, you got here earlier than we did, or you stayed later than we stayed." For several years, I listened to them discuss it while they were standing there looking at my many bags full of mussel shells at the end of the day. Not once did I hear them say it was the bags. They knew I had a rope around my neck on which I hung the bags.

They dragged their bags so they always assumed I did the same thing. This is so important: They missed the big picture by assuming. I think because dragging your bag was the smallest of things to consider, it was the easiest to overlook as simply another excuse.

I often wondered how they could see all my bags of mussel shells and not figure it out. Everything else was the same. Yes, I did get there earlier and stay later, but my bags allowed me to work longer. But I didn't smoke which gave them something to blame. We worked under water with low visibility, so they couldn't see how I used my bags. When they read this book, they'll know.

"Man is a tool-using animal. Without tools he is nothing, with tools he is all."

~ Thomas Carlyle

CHAPTER 4

Worker Relationships
(or Assemble Your Nest)

A significant and crucial key to your success is worker selection. It's better not to hire someone if that person isn't the right fit in your work culture. Much time, effort, and resources can be spent hiring and re-hiring. You should spend three to five times more effort in constructing your interview questions and observations than interviewing itself. You must discern what the interviewee really means and whether he/she is telling you what you want to hear — or simply what he/she thinks you want to hear. Spend time during the interview in the workplace. If you have other workers, involve them during the interview processes and note the interactions between your employees and the interviewee.

Another key to your success is getting the most from your workers — not by demanding, but by demonstrating to them how to be successful. Show them how to be efficient; show them how to work hard and smart. They must realize that you're pulling for them to achieve and to grow in ways that will help them in all parts of their lives — not merely on the job.

Explain to your workers that although you're their friend, you have to be their boss first. For example, teach a good worker how to be a more productive worker. Don't waste your time on a bad worker who isn't willing to learn. It's a waste of your time. It doesn't mean you can't use that person. Just place the individual somewhere so other workers' time isn't wasted or work pace slowed down.

Be the kind of person who inspires people to want to do things for you. Practice being honest, patient, and kind every day. By treating your workers with proper respect, you'll be surprised how workers will help you.

Be a smart boss. Be aware of how your employees perceive you. Be friendly and be on their side. Be serious about the job. Be willing to do any job on the site. Make sure you're serious, even when doing small tasks, relating how important those tasks are in **the big picture**.

You must be able to gauge productivity. Some employees are adept at looking busy, and they may even feel productive. One of your jobs is to teach them the difference between activity and productivity.

Honestly, I backed in to the difference between activity and productivity. Daddy owned a nursery, and during the early years, we used a hoe to kill the weeds. I was meticulous while hoeing, trying to kill every single weed. I perceived, Daddy, on the other hand, as rather sloppy. He hoed at a faster pace and would dig up some weeds and use the same dirt to smother other weeds. I reasoned he had to miss a few while making comparisons of hoeing techniques. But here's the problem, I'd be about 10 yards back down the row as Dad increased his lead to about 25 yards. I wasn't as active as Daddy considering his fast pace, but even worse, I wasn't as productive. I learned, and I must say the hard way, that I had to sacrifice some neatness to increase my productivity. Although I continued to improve, I never could keep up with Daddy.

A healthy environment is critical to business success. Talk to your employees about being positive, especially toward other workers. Saying bad things about other workers causes many problems from low morale to lower productivity.

Watch your employees. You'll learn to tell if they're distracted. They're human and will have problems from time to time. Some people keep their personal lives in a mess, which can easily spill over into their work. Usually, they won't see it hurting their performance. You may be able to help them, maybe not.

Be careful hiring big talkers unless you're hiring them to talk! Seriously, every person believes himself to be a hard worker — even the worst worker.

Help your employees see the big picture — the plan for the day, week, month, and/or season. This will help them realize the importance of doing your job today so that when tomorrow arrives, you can do tomorrow's job. One word of caution, when you employ family members or friends, be careful not to assume they automatically see the big picture. Do you recall my hoeing story? Reflecting on that experience, I'd like to think I would've learned the difference between activity and productivity earlier than I did if Daddy had talked with me about his plans. He knew we had acres and acres of work, so he viewed each day as a process to production. I viewed each day as hard labor, but my vision was getting to lunch or to the end of the day. I simply didn't have the big picture; therefore, my view of work was quite negative. Think long and hard before hiring your friends or family, but if you do hire them, share the big picture with them.

Finally, don't expect too much from workers and watch for them getting burned out. You should plan job rotation, time off, and routine changes to provide worker variety. One of the great things Daddy did was to change routines — anything but hoeing, right? We raised hogs and broiler chickens on our little farm and like most farms, we wasted little. For example, each day we lost a number of our more than 6,000 chickens. We fed the dead chickens to the hogs as supplementary food. Additionally, Daddy had stretched his acreage of trees to the point that some weeds would get knee-high before we could hoe them. Daddy used those weeds for additional supplementary food for our hogs. Of course, I simply welcomed the change to pulling big weeds and loading the truck rather than hoeing. I viewed pulling weeds as a break simply because of the variety it gave me in my workday.

Many of your workers won't see the big picture for a number of reasons. A few may not be able to conceptualize your vision. Some just won't care about the big picture.

Nevertheless, you must take your workers where they are and continue to educate them about your vision for the business. Although I didn't see Daddy's big picture of not wasting a weed, in my innocence or my ignorance, I simply appreciated the break from hoeing.

"The better person you become, the better person you will attract."

~ Zig Ziglar

CHAPTER 5

Perseverance

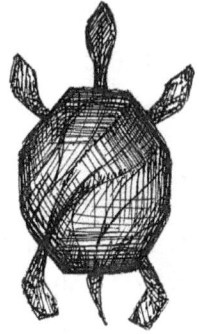

Every successful person, in life and work, has the wonderful trait of perseverance. At times, perseverance may include some stubbornness, blind faith, a refusal to lose, and/or an extreme focus. This trait has been honored since biblical times as a number of stories reveal that people often succeed because of their perseverance.

Focus can help you develop perseverance. Why do you do what you do? How will you measure your productivity for the day? When I dived for mussel shells, I recall some divers kept a short pole tied to their weight belt with a fishhook on the end. If they were diving and encountered a stump with a big catfish lying under it, they would loosen the pole from their weight belt and hook the fish. Of course, they stopped looking for mussel shells while they carried the fish back to the boat, climbed into the boat, unhooked the weight belt, turned off the air compressor, and put the catfish in the live well. Then, they reversed the process and returned to collecting mussel shells.

One day I asked one of them why he was wasting time with that fish. Curiously he asked, "What do you mean? I get a free fish dinner tonight!" I told him he was spending precious time with that fish, and I had picked up enough mussel shells during that time to pay for two fish dinners — already cooked with a baked potato and hush puppies! Because of those big catfish, my friends lost their focus; thankfully, I kept mine. In addition to wasting valuable time handling the catfish, those men also had to keep up with that pole and drag it around all day which probably reduced their productivity as well.

The catfish are plentiful in the river, so my friends were tempted often. Regardless of your field of endeavor, you'll always have your "catfish" (your distractions). Although you must persevere, you also must focus on how you'll measure your productivity that day. Stay focused.

I believe God gives perseverance to each of us. I remember going on a church roller skating trip where I watched Troy, a 4- or 5-year-old youngster, learning to roller skate. Troy couldn't stand up on roller skates . . . much less skate! What I vividly remember, however, is that he immediately got up, fell, got up, fell, got up, fell, got up; well, you get the picture. Seriously, he must have fallen about 300 times that afternoon; however, he got up as quickly — or maybe quicker — each time. After a couple of hours, he was falling less frequently. I remember commenting to his parents that it wouldn't matter what that young man does, he'll succeed in life if he continues to persevere.

Just like in roller skating, all of us fall in life. Successful people view falling as natural and perhaps inevitable; however, they get up quickly. They learn from falling. They persevere.

"It's not whether you get knocked down, it's whether you get up."
~ Vince Lombardi

"Winners never quit and quitters never win."
~ Vince Lombardi

CHAPTER 6

Stupid Is as Stupid Does

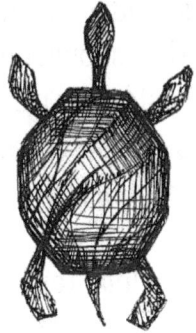

I once hired a concrete worker to pour concrete for me. He told me he wasn't responsible for cracks in the concrete. Having heard his pronouncement, I assumed he would do all he could to prevent it from cracking. I was wrong. He let it dry too fast, and it cracked. When I complained, he stated again, "I'm not responsible for cracks." I told him I assumed he would do all he could to stop it from cracking, and I still think he should have. Furthermore, he should say that and make all attempts to do so.

Of course, he thought he was absolved from responsibility and legally he was. But, but, but ... stupid is as stupid does. The next time I needed concrete, I didn't call him. The next time someone asked me for a good concrete man, I didn't recommend him. The next guys I hired did a great job, so I'll continue to provide them with my business. Though the first guy really did me a favor in the long run, what he did was stupid for his continued business.

One time I was talking to a guy who does carpentry and asked him if he would like to do a particular type of carpentry. He said, "Yeah, we can do it, and we've done it before, but we don't like to do that kind of work." Whew, stupid is as stupid does. From experience I know not to hire someone who doesn't like to work.

All too often, many small business owners seem to think that people with money are gullible, so they try to charge wealthy people more money than they'd charge their typical customer. Not only is this unethical, it's ...

stupid is as stupid does. People with money do a lot of repeat business. They should be the ones of whom you should take special care! Wealthy customers can often make or break a small business. They usually know other potential customers, too, so treat them fairly so that they'll recommend your business to others.

As an entrepreneur, you must view customers and customer service in a long-term perspective.

As an academic, I can attest that students have said many things to me that fall into this "stupid is as stupid does" category. One of the most frequent insults students will ask following an absence is, "Did I miss anything important?" or "Did we do anything important?" Neither of those questions could be more insulting to a conscientious teacher. Diligent teachers convey something "new" in class every day . . . something that will be covered only that day . . . every class day!

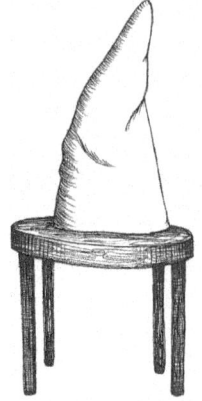

Oh, but it doesn't stop there. Instructors are required to distribute a syllabus for each class with the rules pertaining to the class. You can state explicitly that no make-up quizzes will be given; however, usually within the first three weeks of class, a student will miss and guess what question he'll ask? You guessed it: "When can I make up the quiz?" There's a growing population of students and adults who think the rules apply to everyone *except* them. They picture only themselves and never see the big picture.

Stupid is as stupid does.

> *"We are all born ignorant, but one must work hard to remain stupid."*
> ~ Benjamin Franklin

> *"Life is tough, but it's tougher when you're stupid."*
> ~ John Wayne

CHAPTER 7

A Time for All Things

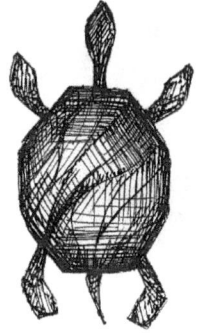

To paraphrase Ecclesiastes 3:1, there is a time for all things. Most of us have heard this adage and have likely heard it read at funerals, during sermons, or spoken at work and in life situations. Although it could be misused as an excuse for not giving 100 percent effort into one's work, have you ever considered its application to excuse sloppiness?

Neatness is an admirable trait *almost* all of the time. Certain situations or events, such as weddings, funerals, and going to church, demand we look our best. But at work, are there times when one shouldn't be neat? Are there times when sloppiness isn't only excused, but pragmatically and economically wise? The answer is yes.

Knowing when to be messy is hard to teach. As you know, some people are messy too often, and others are neat freaks. Teaching a neat freak to "let it go" until a less busy time can be hard to do.

For example, restaurants have busy times. Visualize rush hour at restaurants. The workers are busy providing food and don't have time to sweep and clean floors. Frankly, they should let the place get messy during these hours. Getting customers their food should trump crumbs on the floor. During egg season, we're often so busy collecting turtle eggs that we don't have time to stop and sweep floors. Our facility can get messy sometimes. I have a hard time explaining to our "neat" workers that the messiness is OK when collecting eggs is the priority.

Often you can learn things in life that transfer to your workplace. When I was a child, we went blueberry picking in the summer. My Uncle

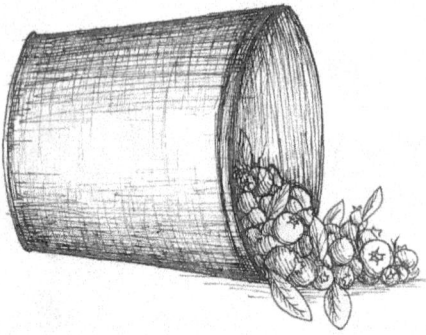

Roscoe taught Daddy and me a lesson one summer. Daddy and I each took a small bucket to fill on our blueberry adventure; it takes a lot of blueberries to fill a bucket! He and I were neat as we picked. We were careful to select only the ripe berries while leaving the green ones. As I recall, we wore out before we ever filled our buckets. We walked miles in those woods hunting berries.

One day, we ran into Uncle Roscoe who was carrying a Number 3 tub! That tub was 90 percent full of blueberries . . . and sticks, and leaves, and some green berries. He asked us what we were doing, and we responded "picking blueberries." As he strolled away toting his Number 3 tub, he was laughing aloud at us.

Now what Uncle Roscoe was doing may not be considered "green" today; however, he probably spent only a fourth of the time we did picking berries. He certainly had more ripe blueberries than we did, but he had just as many green ones he could allow to ripen at home. Uncle Roscoe would place his tub under a blueberry bush and "beat the fire" out of the bush causing leaves, twigs, and berries to fall into his tub. Overall, his being "messy" made him much more productive. Upon arriving home, he would simply fill his tub with water, which allowed the leaf debris and twigs to float to the top; furthermore, he just took his berries through a cleaning wash!

Although Daddy completed only the third grade, I've never met a more "educated" person than he. Having a diploma is one thing; being educated is another issue. Daddy learned to transfer what Uncle Roscoe was doing with blueberries to his nursery business.

Each autumn we would collect berries, acorns, and various types of seeds. We changed our method of picking blueberries, but we also changed our method of picking dogwood berries and other seeds. For instance, we would back up our truck to a dogwood tree and "beat the fire" out of the dogwood tree! Yes, we would get some twigs, leaves, and unripe berries; however, we would get loads of dogwood berries to plant in a fraction of the time! Sometimes, being "messy" really pays off!

Back to the "green" issue — how we gathered those dogwood berries not being green is more apparent than real. Actually, it turns out being "messy" in gathering those berries is quite "green." You see, when we planted the dogwood berries, we simply included the twigs and leaves — composting at its finest! The composting effect of the twigs and leaves increased the germination of the seeds as well as fertilizing the plant. So, Daddy ended up having acres of dogwood seeds which later became plants, which later were lined out into rows of dogwood trees.

Yes, there's a time for all things . . . even a time to be messy.

"Exactness and neatness in moderation is a virtue, but carried to extremes narrows the mind."

~ Francois Fenelon

CHAPTER 8

All That Glitters Is Not Gold

In this country, I've noticed a strange thing concerning economics during my lifetime. Generally speaking, the strange thing is that most people who appear to have money do not, and those who appear not to have money actually do have it!

When I say money, I'm speaking of total assets or net worth. We have a society that judges people's affluence by the house in which they live or even more so by the automobile they drive.

The epiphany hit me one day when I picked up my younger son, Seth, from soccer practice in 2002. He was in middle school, was a pretty good soccer player, and had (and continues to have) a good business sense about him. As I sat in my 1993 Toyota pickup truck, a driver in a beautiful metallic blue, leather rich, new BMW convertible pulled up beside me. I readily admit the car was breathtaking! At the end of practice as Seth climbed into my old pickup truck, he asked, "Dad, when will we be rich like those people?"

Teachers have something they've affectionately termed a "teachable moment" — and here was one of those priceless opportunities for me to teach my son a lesson about economics since he'd asked a question with such depth.

Seth simply assumed what most adults in this country assume today about automobiles — if you drive it, you own it. The truth is that the bank (or finance company) owns many, if not most, of the automobiles you see on the road. So I asked Seth, "What makes you think they're rich?" Duh! Seth said, "Look at that car, Daddy — it's hot!" As a social scientist, I couldn't say whether that particular car was paid for; however, I can tell you that a great percentage of the cars you see on the road aren't paid in full. Seth learned that day his father's old truck was owned by his father, and he learned not to assume that everyone actually owned the vehicle they drove.

Fast forward to 2015. Yes, I'm still driving my 1993 Toyota pickup truck. The truck is 22 years old and has about 225,000 miles on it. The compressor on the air conditioner recently died. As I was having my truck repaired, my boss, Steve, gave me a ride home from work since he lives near us. Steve and I have been friends and colleagues for more than 35 years, and we've had many conversations about money. By the way, Steve drives a 1992 Chevy S-10 pickup truck, and his truck has more mileage than mine!

As Steve drove me home that day, we discussed the economics of gas prices and other things. At one stoplight, I commented, "Steve, I bet some people are looking at you in this old paint-faded truck thinking, *Bless his heart; he can't afford to buy a new truck,*" Steve responded, "You know I could buy (pay cash for) a new truck because I ride in this old truck." And I'm confident he could because he understands that most people have more automobile than they need; furthermore, they go into debt to obtain it. When people borrow money to purchase a depreciating asset, they're wasting money at both ends.

One of the guys who worked for me several years ago and I rode across town in one of my old farm vans with no air conditioning. On the way back, he said, "You know people are laughing at us in this 'old lady' van." I looked over at him and said, "Well, when we get back to the farm, let's wash it — they won't be laughing then." He looked at me like he was wasting his time trying to explain something to me. He evidently didn't understand that the "old lady" van was providing the use my business needed and that I couldn't care less if people laughed.

One time I was at a car dealership looking at new cars, and the salesman told me that his dealership's make of cars wouldn't depreciate in value. I said, "Well, son, if you will put that in writing that a year from now they'll be worth as much as I pay you today or you'll buy them back, I'll take two today." His reply? "You're a smart guy, and you know how it works." I didn't buy a car from him, because I do know how it works.

I tell my sons that salespeople enjoy uneducated buyers, so the more uneducated you are about the item you're buying, the more they enjoy you. I also tell them that anything you buy or sell in a hurry will probably cost you money.

I had an old friend who once told me that buying things to impress others will get you broke in a hurry. I have thought about it many times over the years. When I buy something expensive, I ask myself if I am buying it for the right reason. Although my friend has been dead for several years, I think about him often because of his statement.

No matter what some people buy, they think because they paid a certain amount for it that it's still worth that amount. You must stop thinking that way in business. If you need to buy a car by loan, your goal needs to be to buy the cheapest car that will get you by until you can make a cash purchase. Also keep in mind, if you buy a $5,000 car, the most you can lose is $5,000. If you buy a $50,000 car, you can lose — well, you get the picture! Oh, yes, buy a $50,000 car and drive it for a few years, and you'll be driving a $5,000 car.

Warren Buffet, one of the richest men in America today, lives in a house that most Americans — even young couples — wouldn't consider buying as a "starter" house. Most Americans, and I'm guilty of this too, have more house than they need. At least a house typically increases in value, so borrowing money to get a house is understandable. Borrowing money to buy a depreciating asset like an automobile could go in the "Stupid Is as Stupid Does" chapter (*see Chapter 6*).

While discussing this economic concept with a contractor one day, he told me about his brother. As we talked while he replaced my roof, I could tell he had common sense. He told me his brother was about to go into business for himself and that he was going to borrow $100,000 to do so. His brother consulted him about his business plan which included spending $45-48,000 on a new truck, which would have advertising on it.

My contractor told his brother, wisely I might add, that he needed to spend much less on a truck and create a customer base first! Further, he could advertise on a less expensive truck just as well as a more expensive truck. My contractor's brother had been influenced by our society's view of new automobiles. He was going to spend basically half of his borrowed money on a truck!

Automobiles are probably the biggest "wealth robber" in this country. Purchasing (with borrowed money) the best automobile to impress people prevents millions of people from building wealth. If you use your money to impress others, you're going to be in for a shock. By purchasing (in cash) a less expensive automobile and getting only what you need, you can use the money you save to invest in your business or to build your retirement account — either builds your assets/wealth.

In business, you must think of your money or working capital as a tool (*see Chapter 3*). You must develop the habit of *seeing* money as a tool — where will it work best for you to get where you want to go.

Daddy taught me something years ago that I've never forgotten. We were discussing money one day — particularly being rich. Daddy asked me, "Son, do you know who the richest people in the world are?" Even as a child, I realized he was about to impart some wisdom to me. Daddy said, "The richest people in the world are the ones who need the least." Fifty years later, I find much wisdom in his words. When you consider economic appearance in this country, *all that glitters is not gold.*

"There is no logical way to the discovery of these elemental laws. There is only the way of intuition, which is helped by a feeling for the order lying behind the appearance."

~ Albert Einstein

CHAPTER 9

Go to the Shed

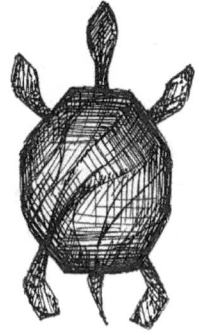

I remember a story about a healthy, muscular young man who went to work for a lumber company cutting timber. He bought the finest ax and reported to work promptly at the start time. He quickly learned of his competition — an older gentleman was also cutting timber for the lumber company.

On the first day with his new ax, he hewed as many trees as the older guy until lunch. Both took their lunch breaks, and the young guy thought he would cut more than the older guy after lunch — he would cut faster. During the lunch hour, the older guy went to a shed and stayed the whole hour. The young guy started back to work 15 minutes early so he could cut a little bit more than the older guy; however, at the end of the day, they had cut about the same number of logs.

On the second day, the young man reported to work 30 minutes early and had cut a few more logs by lunch than the older gentleman. During the lunch hour, the older guy went to the shed again and stayed the whole hour. To the young man's surprise, at the end of the second day, they had cut about the same number of logs.

On the third day, the young man reported to work an hour early and, again, had cut a few more logs by lunch than the older gentleman. During the lunch hour, the older guy went to the shed again and stayed the whole hour. The young man thought he would surely cut more logs today than the older gentleman. To the young man's surprise, the older guy cut more than he could the second half of the day, and they ended with about the same number of logs.

Frustrated, the younger man went over to talk to the older gentleman: "I've started to work before you do, and I don't take an hour for lunch; nevertheless, at day's end we cut about the same number of logs. How is that possible?" The older guy grinned and told him that he ate lunch in the shed, but once he'd finished his meal each day, he sharpened his ax.

As discussed earlier (*see Chapter 3*), tools are important; however, just as important as tools is keeping your tools sharpened or maintained. Like most businesses, the turtle business is seasonal. The time to sharpen/maintain your tools is during the "off" season — whatever that season is for you. We try to have everything in working order before turtle season begins. We don't have time to stop and repair machinery like chainsaws and weed eaters on busy days. Our time is so important during turtle season that I have two of those types of machines. I refuse to let a weed eater or chainsaw stop us from collecting the turtle eggs. Collecting turtle eggs is an essential part of the business and must take priority.

If you have tools, you will have breakdowns! Your goal should be to minimize the interruption when those breakdowns occur. Remember, you want to be the most productive that day rather than spending half of your day repairing a tool.

The danger of thinking of tools as only mechanical or thinking of tools only as "things" that need repair entraps many people. People are also tools! Your body is the main tool you need. I think most people overlook the fact that running a business can really take a toll on your body — mentally, physically, and emotionally. You should consider your body as a tool when constructing your business plan and your to-do list. Many people don't understand that this is a crucial part of running a business. You must get rest! If not, you'll burn out quickly, which can cost your business dearly.

I had a customer in China a few years ago who would call me after my bedtime during the busy season. He knew he had awakened me after a long day, and he wanted to negotiate prices. This tactic gave him a huge advantage while negotiating. I was mentally, physically, and emotionally worn out, so I was more likely to agree to his request. I was too tired to think to my business's advantage; therefore, I was more likely to agree with his request.

When you realize that the main tool (your body) should be in proper working order, you'll understand the importance of getting enough rest. The right foods (fuel) are important for both your working and thinking processes. Remember, you're trying to be the best at what you do. In this respect, you have the same tool as your competitor. Your advantage may be keeping your body in better working condition than your competitor keeps his/hers.

Besides yourself, your employees are your next most vital tool. They're the most expensive tool you will need — either mechanical or personal. Learning how to get the most out of them is your job. Post notes about health, eating and drinking habits, and proper rest important to the human body. You may be surprised how little some workers know about healthcare.

How you communicate this concern is important. Most people won't respond well to your telling them what to eat and drink. People respond much better to a caring approach for their well-being. They respond well to information that educates them as individuals. So post notes about how your body needs water for proper hydration. Lack of water causes dehydration, which causes your kidneys to work harder. Your workplace should have plenty of water sources available to encourage the positive habit of hydration. Instead of telling my workers, I like to post information about healthcare in the breakroom. It's an indirect approach, but it works for me.

What's the bottom line of this chapter? Your body is the most important tool. If your body breaks down, it could bankrupt you. There have been times in my life (particularly the younger years) that I didn't think

my body was that important. Now I know just because my body is working well today doesn't mean it will work well tomorrow. **Go to the shed** — keep your tools, and yourself, properly maintained.

Time can also be considered a tool, one which you'll occasionally need to sharpen.

Be alert for time management seminars and books on time management. Frankly, you have to be an effective time manager to survive as an entrepreneur; however, all of us are too close to see where we may become inefficient with this valuable tool. Just like all of our tools, the time tool must be maintained as well. Allocate time to go to the shed to sharpen your time management tool.

"Managing your time without setting priorities is like shooting randomly and calling whatever you hit the target."

~ Peter Turla

CHAPTER 10

Lend Me an Ear

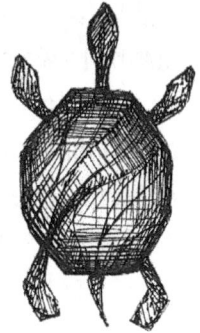

I f you're an entrepreneur about to go into business, some of the toughest questions you have to ask yourself are, "How much money should I borrow? How much is enough? How much is more than I really need? How much will the bank allow me to borrow?"

Furthermore, once you've experienced some success, years later the same questions arise. You need capital to go to the next level for your business success. You'd be normal if you thought your borrowing money is what this chapter is about; however, you'd be mistaken. This chapter puts you on the other side of the desk and supposes that you're the lender. Sooner or later, and it's usually sooner than you think, a supplier or a buyer (or both) will seek credit (money) from you. An employee or renter will seek money (credit) from you. Here are a few stories we've experienced, and we sincerely hope the scenarios assist in preparing you for your "lending" decisions . . . the decision-making will come!

When I was in the mussel shell business, the divers would often ask to borrow money during the winter months to get by when it was too cold to dive. Initially, I thought this was a good deal for me since the divers wouldn't get another job and would need to collect mussel shells for me in the spring. By borrowing money from me, the divers would be financially obligated to me and eagerly collect mussel shells in the spring. So, my intent was to help them and my business.

Two realizations burst that intention. First, once they discovered they could borrow money from me, their winters got longer and longer. They would stop diving earlier in autumn than they previously had and delay starting to work in the spring. By lending them money, I allowed them to work less to get by. When they started working fewer hours, they had to borrow more money to get by. Furthermore, by working fewer days and hours, my inventory supply diminished.

Secondly, since they owed me money when spring arrived, they would dive and sell their mussel shells to my competitor, so they didn't have to pay me. As the winters got longer, and their debts got higher, the more divers I lost to my competitor.

One year I sold some turtles to a customer in Europe on credit. He requested a larger shipment at one time to cut the cost of shipping and to have more inventory on hand to sell quicker. Sounds reasonable, doesn't it?

When I shipped the turtles, the price was at one level. It took longer to sell the turtles than anticipated. Can you guess what happened? By holding the turtles longer, the money saved on shipping was lost on food and labor taking care of them. To make matters worse, the wholesale price dropped, so we lost more money due to time holding the inventory. Did you notice that I said "we" even though I had shipped the turtles to my customer months earlier?

Remember this was a credit sale. Until you get your money, you have basically created a partnership with your customer through your inventory. Another challenge arose because the value of the euro dropped considerably. Do you know what that means? More money was lost because the value of your inventory (to your customer) just dropped. If you plan to do business overseas, you need to understand exchange rates and the value of the dollar.

A friend of mine had a convenience store and hot food deli. He told me he had a good customer who got in a financial bind, so he allowed him to buy about $300 worth of gas and other products on credit. But when the guy got back on his feet, he never mentioned the $300 he owed. One day the store owner asked the guy about it. Guess what happened? His good customer quit coming to the store after that day. So, he not only lost his $300, but he lost a consistent customer as well. I asked him, "What did you do?" He said, "I ran into him at another store and told him to just forget about the $300 and just come back and shop with me. I thought by helping him when he was short of money that he would be my customer forever, but it worked in reverse . . . I almost lost him."

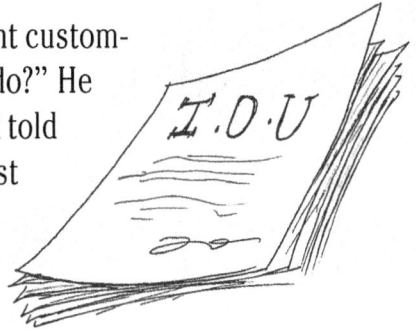

Perhaps you've heard the saying, "The road to hell is paved with good intentions."

Money causes the borrower and lender to view things differently. When you're the lender, time works against you. Even when the borrower has initial good intentions, those intentions may fade over time. The longer it takes to get your money back, the more time there is for something new to happen that was unforeseen, and the less urgency is felt by the borrower.

An old friend once told me, "If someone else has your money, then you are doing something wrong."

We had a rental unit come open in December 2012 . . . just at Christmas time! In hindsight, red flags were waving everywhere, but we all have 20/20 vision looking backward. A lady who had just gone through a divorce wanted to rent our unit; she had a young daughter, her church was helping her out with the first month's rent, and a government agency was helping her out for the next two months' rent. By "then," the divorce would be settled, she would have money from the settlement, and she would be back on her feet. The church had even secured employment for her.

We decided to rent to her as we desired to do the Christian thing, and it was so close to Christmas. Anyone can get down on luck, right? Yes, I prayed about it, but I must tell you God rarely gives me clear answers to such questions. She needed to move in quickly to be settled for Christmas, but she didn't have the deposit for electricity. We paid the electric deposit for her agreeing that she would pay us back — when the divorce was settled. At the moment, she was just down on her luck.

We only offer a year's lease, but she signed it and moved in. As they promised, the church paid the December rent; however, we had spent $350 to provide the electricity, which was to be reimbursed. January and February rents were paid by the government agency. March rolled around and nobody paid the rent. The government agency provided only temporary help, and the renter had already lost the job the church acquired for her. She told me to wait until her tax refund and the divorce settlement were to be delivered in April.

April came, but I didn't receive payment for the rent. The renter explained that her income tax refund had not yet arrived, and the divorce was still in litigation. By this time, I started listening for cues such as "I've got a job" or "I'll pay you partial rent next week" or something.

May became the third month without rent because the renter offered no payment.

The renter stated the church would pay May's rent, but I responded by asking about March and April payments. My wife and I discussed this issue and told the renter that we felt like we had been used. Her response left me dumbfounded; she never refuted that statement. I called the church representative who I met in December, and he was plain spoken telling me the church had no intention of paying May's rent.

By being nice, we had rented to someone who, to my knowledge, has yet to get a job, and still owes us four months' rent. Because it takes a while to evict a renter legally, we've lost more than a third of a year's lease. Monetarily, this mistake has cost us thousands of dollars.

What have we learned? We had rules in renting to people, but we broke our own rules. We have realized why we have the rules in the first place; those rules are to protect us.

Establish your rules, being as flexible as you can, but stick to them. Remember, when you loan people money, you become their partner until it's been repaid. Also remember, when you loan people money, time is against you. Get your money back as quickly as you can.

"The rich ruleth over the poor; and the borrower is servant to the lender."

~ Proverbs 22:7 (KJV)

CHAPTER 11

The Ten O'Clock Scholar

Regardless of the business in which you work, you have routine work responsibilities. In addition to the worker relationships discussed in Chapter 4, you have teaching duties. Your business is unique, and you'll have unique ways of doing things. After you hire employees, you're keenly aware you have to teach (or train) them in the routine procedures and tasks of your business. Most entrepreneurs are quite skilled in these routine areas and teach those routine tasks quite thoroughly.

So sit back and relax — your job is done, right? After all, you've taught them how to do the critical parts of the job. You've stayed nearby (initially) to give positive as well as constructive feedback, and you've gradually loosened the reins as they progressed in proficiency. Based on the positive performance, you realize you've taught your employees well, and it's easy at this point to assume you can delegate all types of work for them to do.

This leap of assumption — which is so easy and logical to make — is where we get a lesson in the importance of not assuming. It's natural for us to think that all people possess the general knowledge that we have. Because your workers demonstrate proficiency in the routine tasks you so brilliantly taught them, it's easy to assume the same proficiency in non-routine tasks. It's even easier to assume this proficiency and knowledge in contract workers you hire.

About 20 years ago, I hired a guy to put up a barbwire fence for me. I went to the co-op to pick up the metal posts, barbwire, concrete, corner posts, and the aluminum clips to hold the wire in position. I knew he grew up in the country, and he said he knew how to put up a fence. When I went to check on him and his crew, he was so proud that he had gotten all the fence posts straight, and the wire was tight! I looked at the fence and back at him. He had put the barbwire on the *outside* of the posts. Trying to be nice, I told him most people put the wire on the inside of the metal post so when the cows push on the fence, it pushes the wire against the post. I thought to myself, *He has to know when a 1,000-pound cow pushes against the wire with just that little aluminum clip holding it, the cow will walk right through the fence.* But he replied, "Well, some people do it that way, but I don't."

I learned not to assume all fences are built the same. Aesthetic fences may have the posts hidden for appearance with the planks on the outside of the posts; however, any farm boy has the general knowledge that practical fences have the planks, barbwire, or other barrier on the inside of the posts to provide support. I guess you can be a country boy but not be a farm boy!

The tendency to make assumptions will also bite you in your personal life. A few years ago, my wife and I lived in a subdivision on a rather small lot. A good friend of ours had a horse barn and told us we could use a section of his pasture for a garden. I was excited since I grew up having gardens. I immediately hired a guy to turn the soil. Afterward, I tilled the soil and removed the grass and weeds. We planted a variety of vegetables, but the story of the cucumbers is a must-read.

We had a couple in this subdivision with whom we had developed a strong friendship. Of course, we shared the news with them about the garden, and the wife (of the couple) simply loved cucumbers and volunteered to pick them with us one day. You guessed it; I assumed she knew what she was doing; however, I soon learned differently. If you weren't raised in the country and know little about cucumbers, you need to know two vital things:

1) Cucumbers grow on the ground and bear from vines, and
2) Never step on the vines as you reap early cucumbers to ensure

the vines will bear more vegetables.

This lady was cute as a button — about 5' 2" and was a ball of fire. She hit that cucumber patch with a vengeance and began picking cucumbers feverishly. The problem? She was walking over practically every vine. Yes, she got her cucumbers that day, but she destroyed any future crops by killing the vines.

Another story involves our younger son's girlfriend (at the time). Every late spring or early summer, our family always went to a strawberry farm to pick strawberries. Everyone in our family thoroughly enjoys fresh strawberries. Each year area farmers plant a field of strawberries and charge various amounts for different sizes of containers, but you get to pick your own strawberries. The girlfriend wanted to go with us, and we readily agreed. It would be a family outing! If you've picked strawberries before, you know it's a back-challenging endeavor. You either bend your back to pick or you get on all fours or both to save you from later back pain. You do this because strawberries are quite delicate, and you must place the strawberries in your container gently. Everyone knows that right? Wrong! This young lady started picking strawberries and throwing her berries in the container. She may have saved herself some steps, but she was destroying the strawberries.

Lastly, teach your workers. It's so easy to assume they know what you know, but you're the experienced one. I recall an incident when my older son, Shayne, was ready for his first lawn-mowing job on the riding lawn mower. As I was taking care of other yard work, I casually told him to gas it up, and I would come over and tell him the steps to get it started. Now my riding lawn mower is a four-cycle engine, and I had both two-cycle and four-cycle tanks of gas.

Of course, I knew how the tanks differ, but how could my son know? I gave him a glance and was shocked as he was pouring two-cycle gasoline into a four-cycle tank. I remember I fussed on him a bit, and now I'm ashamed of it. I should have taught him the difference between four- and two-cycle engines before delegating the work to him.

My younger son, Seth, learned a lesson a few years ago about assum-

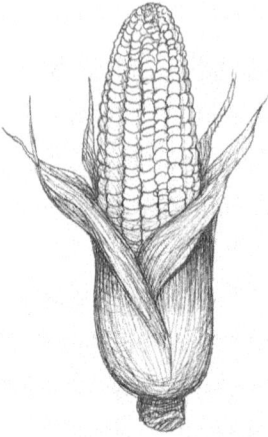

ing his friends had the general knowledge he had. He was with his friends one day in his high school years. These were friends with whom he hung out, played ball, and shared much time. They lived in the same town, went to the same school, and played ball on the same teams. Daddy had just given me 144 ears of corn, so on my way home, I called Seth to tell him to meet me at home to help me shuck corn. When he told his friends why he had to go, they had no idea what he was talking about. Why should they? When you purchase or see your parents purchase corn from the supermarket all of your life, you have no need to shuck corn. Of course, Seth explained to them what shucking corn meant, but he was astounded they didn't know. The only reason Seth knew was because his grandpa grew corn; therefore, he had the general knowledge.

Remember, you're the knowledgeable one in your business. Although you realize you must teach routine tasks and procedures, be careful assuming that your workers have general knowledge that you possess. Often, they may even "think" they know, but you need to ask key questions to validate their knowledge. The safest way is to demonstrate the task/procedure, whether it's pouring in two- or four-cycle gasoline to picking cucumbers to shucking corn to putting up fences!

You will always be teaching and learning. Your workers will always be learning, and your workers will always be making mistakes. You simply hope your employees' mistakes become more infrequent and minor in nature. We hope the same for ourselves!

"If you're not making mistakes, then you're not doing anything. I'm positive that a doer makes mistakes."
~ John Wooden

CHAPTER 12

For Better, For Worse

As we wrote this chapter, we hesitated to engrave any business rule in stone. Day-to-day business has a way of changing every day. The rules change, too. Changing rules is another reason why it's so important for you to look at **the big picture** when problems head your way. You, along with your spouse, may make many rules as you go, only to change those rules as you both learn and feel your way to successful business management.

The importance of your spouse might be easy to overlook at first glance. If you plan to be married and have a business, I hope some of these thoughts will be helpful. Simply stated, your spouse is the vice president in charge of any and everything.

The partner you picked to be your perfect spouse may not necessarily be the perfect business partner for you. Though an employee can usually leave work at the office, this is seldom the case for the business owner. Whether or not your spouse has a title in the business, he or she will become a part of the business. For the business owner, it's often impossible to separate business and personal hours.

Most people don't realize it, but being the spouse of a driven entrepreneur or business person is a trying road. Everyone has heard that behind every successful man is a good woman. There is much truth to that. It's extremely important to talk with your spouse about your business plans. Don't assume that your spouse is on board with all of your business plans. He or she may have different goals and different ideas. It's essential to discuss the business plans with your spouse beforehand.

The role your spouse plays may vary widely from day-to-day. Often, the business owner simply needs moral support. At other times, the spouse may be needed to help with basic operations or run errands — everything from operating the register to picking up office supplies to cleaning the office restroom! Sometimes it may be the little things your spouse does that help the most (*see Chapter 1—It's the Small Things*). It could be, at those times, when the spouse is helping with jobs that might seem menial, that he or she could most use a few words of appreciation for the help. Thank your spouse for big and small tasks completed.

There may be times when your spouse can best help by listening, to you vent about your frustrations. Your spouse doesn't have to offer a solution, just a willing and patient ear. You'll most likely welcome any solutions your spouse can offer.

It's important for your spouse to realize that in most startup businesses, a time clock doesn't exist. "Nine to Five" doesn't exist. New businesses need new customers. Obtaining new customers often means working around the customers' time clocks. That could mean 7 a.m. to 7 p.m. and beyond. This time demand could vary from season-to-season, depending on the type of business you choose.

Expecting your spouse to be able to do everything perfectly is unfair. Your main goal for your spouse's involvement should be for him or her to fill in where the business needs are. It's also important to remember that while your spouse may often fill the same roles as the employees, your spouse is also your partner. The dialogue between spouses (partners) is different than the communication between an employer and employee.

Lastly, it's important to agree at the onset of your venture that whether you succeed or fail, you're in this together. Finger pointing in the event of a problem is counterproductive. You're a team — literally.

Other comments that aren't helpful and can cause deeper problems include:

"I told you that wouldn't work!"

"What were you thinking?"

"Why did you do it *that* way?"

"I told you that person wasn't trustworthy."

"I would have never done it like that!"

It goes without saying that name-calling and assigning blame after the fact is off-limits and is unproductive. Once a problem has arisen, it doesn't help to list all the ways it could have been prevented. Now is the time to find solutions. When tempers are cooled and humor has returned, it might be good to discuss ways to prevent a repeat problem. Especially when working with your spouse, look for **the big picture**.

> *"A happy home is one in which each spouse grants the possibility that the other may be right, though neither believes it."*
> ~ Don Fraser

> *"Pray for your mate. Ask God to soften your heart and show you ways to be a better spouse."*
> ~ Willie Aames

> *"Brands mature over time, like a marriage. The bond you feel with your spouse is different than when you first met each other. Excitement and discovery are replaced by comfort and depth."*
> ~ Gary Vaynerchuk

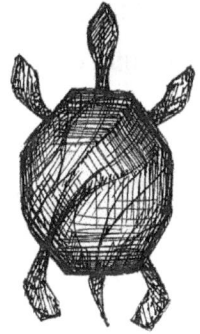

CHAPTER 13

To Tweet or Not To Tweet

It's easy to miss the big picture of technology in the workplace. Modern technology has increased productivity in significant ways and has increased personal convenience. It's so easy to check one's Facebook status, to send a text message, to tweet at a moment's notice, to take a photograph, to conduct your banking, and even shop online with your smartphone, which coincidentally can still be used for having an actual conversation.

We live in the technology age. Many employees have smartphones and have access to various social media, text messages, and phone calls. Although having a smartphone is a huge convenience, it can also be costly to a business. This chapter isn't about emergency phone calls which employees have always had and will always have. This chapter is about employee abuse of technology on company time.

I hear employees saying:

"I was only on the phone five minutes."

"I just had to answer a text real quickly."

"I am laughing because I just saw something funny on my Facebook page!"

"I'm going shopping tonight so I had to check my bank account balance on my phone."

"There is an auction running on E-bay, and I had to make sure I wasn't being outbid!"

These are just a few of the comments you may hear now in many workplaces regarding personal technology being used during work hours. Most employees will tell you they were on their phone fewer than five minutes. Let's look at the big picture of technology in the work place.

When you break this down into how much time is really lost from each interruption to the work day, the loss is much more than you might think. If you consider the 5-10 minutes for the interruption, and then the 20-30 minutes it takes the employee to get the proper mindset to get back to the task at hand, this employee has now taken 20-30 minutes from productive work. Depending on the type of interruption, the employee may be distracted much longer if the topic was upsetting. At this rate, two interruptions per day could easily take up 60 minutes of the employee's time. These interruptions, during an 8-hour shift, have cost the employer one hour of productivity—1/8 of the work day! This is even more frightening when you consider 1/8 work day times the number of employees at the business five days in the week.

Let's examine a much bigger picture. Let's say the employee (above) has to share the news or explain the interruption to the nearest work buddy (or buddies). Now the process starts again times two or three! You do the math! The larger the number of employees a company has, the more this "news" costs the company.

Also, if employees are salespeople, they may have lost a sale during this time. Have you ever taken your time to drive to a store to buy something? You walk in ready to purchase the item you're seeking. About the time you ask for help, the phone rings! It can sometimes feel as if the world stops so the employee can answer the phone. Many employees leave ready-to-pay customers standing unassisted while they talk to someone on the phone who may or may not buy anything. Something about phone technology gives most people a false sense of urgency.

This false sense of urgency is prevalent today, especially in the classroom. Today's students have a difficult time listening since they seem unable to disconnect from their phones. Could we say that about society as a whole? Technology in the classroom is wonderful when it's directed. An issue may arise in class discussion, and it's convenient to be able to Google to get an answer promptly. The problem is that many students will be checking their texts, email messages, tweets, etc. and miss the answer.

We have a growing number of people with a condition: They aren't mentally present where they're physically present. They live vicariously somewhere else through media. This condition isn't only detrimental to productivity in the work place but also to learning in the classroom; furthermore, it can be a safety hazard in the work environment.

As an employer or teacher, you cannot stop technology; however, you must learn to manage it. You ignore technology at your peril. Trying to police everyone's smartphone use could create a tense work/classroom environment. An open dialogue setting parameters for media usage is needed in work/classroom environments today. You'll have many employees or students who will find it difficult to turn off media for extended periods; however, productive work and academic learning require it.

"One machine can do the work of fifty ordinary men. No machine can do the work of one extraordinary man."

~ Elbert Hubbard

"Technological progress has merely provided us with more efficient means for going backwards."

~ Aldous Huxley

"The march of science and technology does not imply growing intellectual complexity in the lives of most people. If often means the opposite."

~ Thomas Sowell

"Everybody gets so much information all day long that they lose their common sense."

~ Gertrude Stein

"Getting information off the Internet is like taking a drink from a fire hydrant."

~ Mitchell Kapor

"It has become appallingly obvious that our technology has exceeded our humanity."

~ Albert Einstein

CHAPTER 14

Too Good to be True?

I tried a few business ideas as a young adult, most of which were on the side. I had other income, and my eggs weren't in one basket. But my first real business endeavor (especially concerning risk) isn't one to brag about. So, I'm certainly not bragging, but a major purpose of this book is to help readers do smart things and not do unwise things. I sincerely hope that sharing my mistakes might help you avoid these experiences.

So you have a business idea??? Can you say *bankruptcy?* Well, that is how my first real business venture ended. Let me tell you some of the things I did wrong even before I opened my door for customers.

First, in trying to convince myself this business was a good idea, I asked all the wrong people for advice. I have learned in my business life that asking the wrong people for direction is the biggest mistake most people make. I was so excited about my plans that I started asking friends and family what they thought. They were excited for me so they subconsciously gave me the answers I wanted to hear. You can have the best friends and family, but that doesn't mean they have the proper knowledge or experience to give you sound business advice. People naturally want to help you, but you have to be sure their eagerness to help you doesn't send you in the wrong direction.

Remember, these are your plans so you alone are responsible to make the right decisions. Good or bad, you will carry the results. Find the right people and the right places to get the best advice. I have found that experienced bankers and business attorneys provide sound business advice and opinion. They have witnessed many business plans play out. You may also find that your excitement may make hearing negative advice hard to swallow. Remember, look for the big picture.

Second, I wanted to start my own business so badly that I ignored all the red flags. Upon reflection, they were flying high and popping in the wind. I was so confident that if I could just get into business for myself, I could make it work.

Third, you must examine your timing (*see Chapter 2*). Timing is important in a business sense but also in a personal sense. I was the sole bread winner at that time, and my current job provided our medical insurance. My wife was pregnant with our second child. Assess your timing, both in a business sense and family perspective.

Fourth, I quit my job to run the business. Not only did I lose my income, I then had to take an income out of the new business which put an extra expense on the back of the new business.

Fifth, although I had worked in retail management for years, I had never worked in the restaurant business. Yes, I bought a business to run myself that I knew little about. The hard lesson that I learned is that all retail businesses don't operate under the same management rules. It was easy to think retail management is retail management, and everybody has to eat! What a business — it's too good to be true!

Sixth, I went into debt. I borrowed money to open a business that I knew little about. This step actually has two parts: 1. Know that you know your business; 2. Avoid debt!

Seventh, I assumed that because it was an existing business that it was making money.

I was wrong. I purchased a Profit/Loss statement that wasn't worth the paper on which it was written. I had an accountant go over the statement provided by the previous owner. In short, I did my financial planning by a worthless set of figures. My inexperience and eagerness made me an easy target for a shady business man. They are out there. Be prepared.

Eighth, the restaurant was inside an indoor mall. I didn't realize until later that being inside a mall gave me virtually no advertising power. It's extremely difficult for a small business in a mall to draw customers from outside the mall. All the banners I put up in front of the restaurant were visible only to the customers already in the mall.

Finally, I bought a hamburger restaurant in a mall food-court. Guess what type of business was across the aisle in the mall? Yes, I competed with a major hamburger chain.

Restaurants require a lot of labor to operate, so labor costs are high. Food, as you know, has an expiration date. If you don't sell your food within a set time period, you "eat" the cost when you throw the food out. Also, your employees can give away most, if not all, of your profits if you don't have your procedures down to a science! Extra fries, cheese, pickles, drink re-fills, large servings for medium orders, etc. are often culprits to no profit. When workers add more food than the appropriate amount, that cost falls on you. Employee theft is certainly a concern in the restaurant business, but untrained employees giving away your profits is even more costly.

Well, hindsight is 20/20, and I hope this chapter helps you see your red flags. If something seems too good to be true . . . it probably is!

"A smart man makes a mistake, learns from it, and never makes that mistake again. But a wise man finds a smart man and learns from him how to avoid the mistake altogether."
~ Roy H. Williams

"Even a mistake may turn out to be the one thing necessary to a worthwhile achievement."
~ Henry Ford

"The great mistake you can make in life is continually fearing that you'll make one."
~ Elbert Hubbard

CHAPTER 15

Got The Money, Honey

I recall a country song featuring the lyric, "If you've got the money, honey; I've got the time." Everyone has time, but a lot of people don't have the money. Although the purpose of this book is to help you become successful in business, you must also be successful in your personal life. How you handle your money is a major contributor to success, or failure, in both your business and personal lives. Poor financial management in either your business or personal budget will retard, and often prevent, your success.

We aren't financial counselors, and we've made money mistakes; however, we have learned many rules along the way. Some of these rules we learned easily, but some rules we learned by life's hard knocks. We can only testify that the rules below have worked for us, and we've observed how they have worked for other people. Sadly, what both of us have observed much more frequently is how the violation of these rules has robbed people of potential wealth.

The rules below will help you see the big picture of economics in your personal and business budgets. Simply stated, the way to build wealth in a capitalistic system is to build capital.

Rule #1—Avoid Debt

A few financial gurus will tell you never to go in debt; frankly, that's sound advice. Most people reading this book, however, will have already violated the rule. Are they doomed if they violate this rule? No!

The first question asks why you're in debt. The second question asks how quickly you can get out of debt.

Several business and personal situations justify debt (credit), but you always need to have a plan on how to pay the debt and when it will be paid off — the sooner the better. The personal debt that is justified is your house. Of course, it would be ideal to pay cash for it; however, many people choose to invest in a house rather than paying rent. Historically, the houses purchased *appreciate* in value; an appreciating asset is a debt justification.

Simple? Not really. Three problems typically occur when people go in debt to buy a house. The first problem is the time length of the loan. Financial institutions will be happy to give you a 30-year mortgage which is basically half of your adult life! Sacrifice and save to get a 15-year mortgage; then pay yourself the payment for the remaining 15 years. The second problem is a variable rate, which sounds good when the rate is low, but it can and eventually will increase. Get a fixed rate so you can budget concretely. The third problem is that most people buy more house than they need. When purchasing a house, take an honest examination of your wants versus your needs.

If you're seeking more justifications for debt, you won't find them here. The following examples are "criminal" violators of Rule #1:

- credit card debt
- vacation debt
- automobile debt
- education debt
- appliance debt

Rule #2—Develop the Saving Habit

Many people are unable to save because they already have so much debt. They may possess a "criminal" violator or tragically several of them. So, get out of debt and avoid it like the plague in your future. You must begin to save money, and saving must become a habit.

Once debt is removed (or has a planned removal), only then can you save money to build your emergency fund. Many financial advisors will suggest six months of expenses for an emergency fund.

The emergency fund is to offset "Murphy's Law" when it visits you, and you will be visited by Mr. Murphy. When you need tires for your automobile, when your refrigerator dies, when your television quits working, you need to pay cash for those items — you can with your emergency fund!

Save enough money so that you can buy your next automobile. Notice that automobile debt is on the "criminal" list! The average American simply has a love affair with the automobile. Remember when buying a house, try to buy only what you need. To buy only what you need doubly applies to automobiles. Most Americans have much more automobile than needed, and they dearly pay for it. Automobiles are probably the biggest robbers of wealth-building in this country. Many people not only have car payments, but they also become accustomed to budgeting those payments and keep them for decades as they move from one car payment to another. What a tragic way to squander wealth!

Once you become disciplined enough to pay cash for your next automobile, you'll find yourself probably looking at used (pre-owned) ones since automobiles depreciate in value. You should also realize that the purpose of an automobile is to get you from point "A" to point "B." If you're still status-seeking and wanting to impress your neighbors with your automobile, you're going to be disappointed in your long-term financial status because you're spending money now on value-depreciating transportation.

Credit card debt is a red flag that you're living beyond your means. You're doing the opposite of saving. If you cannot pay off your credit card debt each month, destroy them before they destroy you. You must begin to save money.

Everyone likes vacations, and we wish vacations for everyone; however, you must pay for vacations as you take them. If you can't pay cash for a vacation, don't take it. Besides, vacations are more psychological than physical. Must you spend thousands of dollars to have fun? Examine vacation opportunities that are inexpensive, such as hiking or visiting state and national parks.

Although one of us is a professional, career educator, getting an education on borrowed money is a poor economic way to start a career. We realize that in today's world going to college on a loan is the normal way to get an education; we also realize that most normal people are broke because they've accrued so much debt. Pay for your education as you go; you'll be a much better student and a debt-free graduate.

Rule #3—Get Properly Insured

To protect our loved ones (and our assets), all of us need health insurance, automobile insurance, home insurance, life insurance, disability insurance, and long-term health care insurance. Talk with your agent to discuss the different options of coverage and premiums.

Rule #4—Develop the Giving Habit

From a cognitive perspective, this rule is counter-intuitive! Ironically, this rule will help you see the big picture more than any other rule. You should give 10-15 percent of your income, time, and service to your religious organization and/or to your community — expecting nothing in return. Such giving keeps us from becoming greedy. Giving develops the best part of humans. Giving increases our compassion and prevents pessimism.

Rule #5—Build Your Retirement

The earlier you begin to build your retirement, the more "time" becomes your partner.

One of us is an entrepreneur, and an entrepreneur has various retirement plan options for the business owner as well as for business employees. One of us is a professional who has participated in 403(b), 401(k), and various IRA plans. You need to get a financial advisor to discuss the various ways you can invest in your retirement.

Rule #6—Establish Your Will

You need a will to protect the assets you've spent your life building. You will also possess things that you desire specific people to have upon your death. Although you can go online and purchase "cookie cutter" wills, why risk your estate by taking a chance of forgetting something? We suggest you obtain a lawyer and do this rule professionally.

Plan your financial work, and work your financial plan.

CHAPTER 16

Are We There Yet?

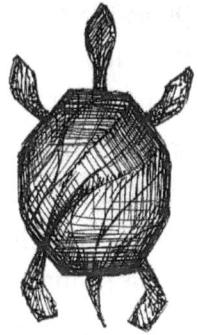

Most of us have traveled on long trips in automobiles with children and heard the familiar phrase, "Are we there yet?" We can be so eager to get somewhere that we miss the joy in the journey.

When you become an entrepreneur, you're on an exciting trip. By reading this book, you've demonstrated you're seeking knowledge, techniques, and tips that will increase the probability of your success.

As stated in the Foreword, identify where you want to be so you can be the first one there. But, are we there yet? Of course not. As you've probably already discovered, "there" keeps changing. Your goals change as you learn, grow, and mature.

Most people begin planning their trips with a map that shows various routes to the desired destination. Is the shortest way always the best way? Often, longer routes are more scenic, and you may want to experience a few attractions on your trip. You may experience rough gravel roads, two-lane roads, and interstate highways. You may have to pay some toll to travel on certain roads. Your entrepreneurial journey will probably have all of those roads as you encounter the challenges of being a business owner.

Nevertheless, plan your route as best you can, taking in the attractions you desire to experience on the journey. You know to keep your tools sharp. In other words, you maintain your major travel tool, the automobile. You double check the tires, the oil level, spare tire inflation, plugs/distributor, air conditioning, various belts, the battery, and other essentials for trouble-free traveling.

Just like in business, your body is the most important tool when you travel. You must have rest, so plan many trips by availability of hotel accommodations. Include your family, especially your spouse, in the travel routes as well – just like you do in your business.

Be prepared for surprises in business just like a toll road may surprise you during your travel. Of course, things will go wrong in business just like a flat tire or an over-heated radiator in your travels. Just as those with a heavy foot end up speeding during their travels, you may find yourself wanting to go too fast in your business. You may end up with fines in both situations when you circumvent the law.

You will learn to make adjustments in your travel plans, just as you learn to make adjustments in your business recipe for success. We believe that not only will the variety of ingredients for your recipe of success change, but the amount of each ingredient will change, too. We earnestly hope that you learned from the stories in this book, but we also hope you have enjoyed reading them. We also hope you'll want to reread the stories periodically as your journey takes you to another "Are we there yet?" moment.

Are we there yet? As you reach intermediate destinations, we trust you'll adjust your itinerary to enjoy some stops along the way! We wish you success in your business and personal endeavors.

Enjoy the trip!

ALABAMA TURTLE FARMER
GARY BENTLEY

Contact the Alabama Turtle Farmer

To find out the latest on the Alabama Turtle Farmer
and the Professor, visit:

alabamaturtlefarmer.com

Gary Bentley is the Alabama Turtle Farmer a motivational humorist that speaks on the topics of:
Roaches to Riches: Story of the Alabama Turtle Farmer
Motivation to Innovation: An Entrepreneur's Journey
And
The Big Picture of Business.

He can deliver a keynote, half-day, or full-day version of his content, depending on your needs. If you are interested in finding out more, please visit alabamaturtlefarmer.com

You can also connect with Gary here:
Twitter:
https://twitter.com/ALturtlefarmer

Facebook:
https://www.facebook.com/alabamaturtlefarmer

WAYNE ROLLINS